# Endorsements

I have known Juliet for nine years. Together, we have shared our hearts, prayed, celebrated birthday dinners, and attended home groups. In all of this, I have watched her walk through a journey of inner healing. Juliet has walked and lived the very pages of this book. She has stepped into inner healing and freedom and, through this book, invites us all along on a journey of healing too. It is filled with Scripture and personal testimonies. I believe that as you read this, you will find glimpses of your own life and step into new freedom from the inside out.

*— Julie Meyer, Worship Leader, International House of Prayer, Kansas City*

The restoration of the body, soul, and spirit is something the Lord strongly desires for all believers. It's rare to find material on the subject of emotional trauma that includes the reality of spiritual involvement. There is a direct connection between one's spiritual life and emotional well-being. It is impossible to receive or maintain emotional stability without addressing our need for spiritual maturity or even deliverance. This workbook is a great resource for both those seeking the restoration they need emotionally as well as a practical tool for spiritual insight and growth. Written with clarity, this book also makes for an effective way to teach and instruct others in the ministry of inner healing. If you have a passion for seeing others healed, or you yourself need healing, I fully recommend this book.

*— Stephen Beauchamp, Director, Deliverance Ministry, International House of Prayer, Kansas City, and Instructor, International House of Prayer University, Kansas City*

Juliet has chosen a vital few elements of inner healing so you don't have to choose from the trivial many that can distract you and prolong your journey to freedom in Christ.

*— Chris Hogan, President, Noble Call Institute*

Juliet Canha tells it like it is: true heart transformation requires that we pass through the grid of the cross. She writes from a heart of compassion and from her own experience on the healing journey. The study questions after each chapter will help equip you to receive the life-changing truth of God's Word.

*– Mike Rizzo, Staff, International House of Prayer, Kansas City*

This book will help you discover the simple, yet powerful, truths for healing in God's Word. Juliet Canha shares clearly and succinctly, helping you discover the path of emotional healing and wholeness in Christ. It is thorough and easy to read. I loved the questions that help one embrace each step of truth along the way. Let this manual guide you as you use the tools provided to allow Jesus and the Holy Spirit to change you and shape you into your true identity – a person made fully alive in Christ!

*– Linda Hackett, Director, Moms' Ministry, International House of Prayer, Kansas City*

# Spiritual Wholeness And Emotional Comfort

---

*A workbook to aid in the journey of healing, freedom, and reaching your potential*

**Juliet Canha**
**Ph.D., Christian Counseling**

**This workbook can be
ordered on Amazon.com and
through other retailers.**

# Acknowledgements

I would like to acknowledge some very significant people whom God has used in my life and in the process of writing this book.

The first person is my husband, Randy Canha. His strength of character and godly example of servanthood to me and our children has deeply impacted my heart. God has used him, through the nearly three decades of our marriage, to help mend the broken pieces of my past by bringing stability and security into my life.

Next, I would like to acknowledge my mother, Shirley Shafer. She, too, has been such a servant to my family and me. Her sweet nurturing heart and sacrificial love have always been such a blessing. I honor her for so faithfully shielding me from many painful things our family had to face while I was growing up.

I would also like to acknowledge my mother-in-law, Carolyn Canha, for generously offering to pay to have this book published. I may never have done it without her encouragement!

I am also very grateful for my dear friend, Shawn Lynch. God brought her into my life when I needed a true friend to stand with me through all of my brokenness. Shawn and her husband, Brian, have impacted my life for eternity with their dedication to our friendship. They have served me and my family in such significant ways. Shawn assisted me with the formatting and editing of this book, and I could not have done it without her!

# Table of Contents

# Foreword

Spiritual wholeness and emotional comfort are two sides of the same coin – our humanity as God intended from the beginning. We cannot make progress toward attaining one side of this coin without courageously pursuing the other. Meanwhile, the world seems to be doing everything it can to prevent both! As we move through this life, we are bumped and bruised along the way. Too often, we simply try to move on without ever taking time (or even knowing how) to recover from the pain inflicted by the circumstances we encounter.

In *Spiritual Wholeness and Emotional Comfort,* Juliet Canha offers recovery "know-how" through sound biblical teaching and insight. The questions and instructions at the end of each chapter are challenging and penetrating, presenting the reader with opportunity to discern the cause of spiritual wounds and emotional distress and receive healing and peace through the declaration of biblical truth. It will be up to the reader to take the time necessary to walk through the healing process. Never fear! You have a loving and compassionate Friend in the Holy Spirit.

*– Tom Mills, Instructor, International House of Prayer University*

# Introduction

The cross is a symbol of death. When our Lord Jesus surrendered to the will of His Father by yielding to unjust treatment and crucifixion, He became the perfect example of love and forgiveness. His death and resurrection paved the way for His Holy Spirit to live in our hearts, enabling us to know God in a real and personal way. God desires that the cross of Christ and His abiding presence within us become our main source of spiritual wholeness and emotional comfort.

This truth started to take root in me around the time that I began taking various classes related to inner healing. About that time, a friend of mine had a spiritual dream about me, which impacted my spiritual and emotional healing. It became an anchor to my soul. The message was: **"Remember Jesus on the cross and find the Spirit within, so you will not be anxious."** When my friend shared her dream with me, I did not have a context for understanding its meaning, but I wrote it down in my journal, respecting my friend's intimate walk with God. Several months later, a very devastating situation occurred in my life, and, at just the right time, the Holy Spirit reminded me about the dream and opened my eyes to the depth of its meaning.

Since that time, I have been learning that a sincere willingness to die to self and yield to the comforting presence of the Holy Spirit is vital for genuine and lasting inner healing. This devotional/workbook is designed to not only take the reader on his or her own inner healing journey, but to also provide insight for helping others through the use of effective prayer ministry tools.

# Chapter 1

## Maintaining an Open Heart

"People need people to recover."[1] When our hearts are closed to others in an effort to prevent further pain, they are also locked to God. This condition not only makes us vulnerable to the enemy's lies, it also prevents us from receiving the healing, love, and comfort we need and find in community. Since a closed heart ("relational circuits" off) can hinder the flow of these life-giving interactions, this first chapter presents important strategies for keeping our hearts open and relating with others at the heart level.

### Relational Circuits

Dr. Karl Lehman (www.kclehman.com) has created a "Relational Circuits Connection Test" that helps to determine when a person's relational circuits are off:

1. Do I feel connected to (name/s)?
2. Do I feel desire to be connected to (name/s)?
3. Do I experience him/her as a unique, valuable, relational being?
4. Am I aware of his/her true heart?
5. Do I feel concern/compassion regarding what he/she thinks and feels?
6. Do I experience his/her presence as a source of joy – or as a problem to be solved or a resource to be used?
7. Am I glad to be with him/her?

If you answer "no" to any of these questions, your relational circuits are off. Everything with respect to your relational conflict will resolve better and more quickly once your relational circuits are reconnected.

In the following paragraphs, my friend, Shawn Lynch, shares the understanding she has gained about relational circuits, based on her own journey of learning how to keep her heart open:

When our circuits are "off", we are unlikely to be able to discern God's voice clearly since this means that we may be disconnected from Him as well as from others. Without access to God (or others), our primary source of information becomes our heart. God's word tells us in Jeremiah 17:9 that our hearts, when allowed to follow their natural inclinations, are deceitful (insincere or intentionally misleading): "The heart is deceitful above all things, and desperately wicked; who can know it?" According to Dictionary.com, deceit is "the quality that prompts intentional concealment or perversion of truth for the purpose of misleading."

Jeremiah's rhetorical question, "Who can know (understand or fathom) it?" warns us that we know very little about our hearts and how they operate. I imagine that if Jeremiah were to elaborate, he would say something like, "Don't be fooled. You have no idea how sneaky your heart is." Since we can't rely on ourselves (our hearts) to "be honest", it is possible we may not answer accurately Dr. Lehman's relational circuits test questions. At least I have found this true for myself. I remember a time when I was aware of a "bad feeling" but unable to recognize this feeling meant that I didn't "feel connected" or "desire to be connected" to someone. (Of note, this experience was during a Thrive conference, where a primary focus is on learning how to check relational circuits!) Looking back, I realize that a combination of pride and shame had made it difficult for me to admit my "bad attitude".

Hidden pride and shame are powerful hindrances to being honest about how we are feeling and what we are really thinking. If negative emotions (e.g., shame) and/or sinful conditions (e.g., pride or bitterness) are present, our hearts probably won't want to "come clean" and admit that we don't want to connect. Often we know instinctively that sin may be involved, but admitting sinful thoughts and attitudes is painful. A deceitful heart will avoid such pain. I have found that it is sometimes easier to "agree" that something is off in how I am feeling than to go head on and admit I have a sinful attitude. With this in mind, some of the "symptoms" I have learned to recognize include:

- Feeling "bad", perhaps not knowing why, and/or not being able to recognize the emotion
- Feeling agitated, unsettled, or unable to relax
- Feeling self conscious, rejected, fearful, judged, or lonely around others
- Feeling irritated or frustrated
- Finding yourself not wanting to attend events involving interaction with people – making excuses; feeling obligation or dread, even starting to feel ill (if you do attend, later you are glad you went, meaning your circuits eventually turned on)
- Being easily irritated with, overly critical of, or quick to judge others over minor issues (unable to "bear with love" and "prefer" others)
- Struggling with feelings of envy toward or competition with others
- Feeling the need to ask Dr. Lehman's relational circuits test questions (if you perceive you need to ask, your circuits are probably off)

This list is somewhat progressive. That is, first I become aware of feeling bad. Once I recognize how I am feeling, I begin asking God why I'm feeling this way. As my heart slowly starts to open to God, my awareness of what's going on with my heart starts to become clearer. At this point, choosing to forgive an offense or letting go of other sinful attitudes may be needed. Soon, my relational circuits are back on. Whether we answer relational questions or note how we are feeling, what is important is that we make the choice to tune in to the indicators that help us recognize when we are disconnected. Then we can take our condition to God, where we can repent if need be and receive God's comfort (see Dr. Lehman's steps below).

Dr. Lehman's steps to restore Relational Circuits are as follows:

1. My goal is to perceive the Lord's presence, tell Him about my pain, and receive His attunement so I can get my relational circuits back on line. (My goal is not to fix the problem that is upsetting me or even resolve underlying trauma.)
2. I talk to God about my emotions and thoughts, even if I don't perceive His presence. (I do not talk to God about the person who is upsetting me as that keeps my relational circuits off.)

3. I invite the Lord to be with me in my pain, asking Him to help me perceive His presence.

## Attuning for Heart-to Heart Communication

To develop a greater degree of trust in our relationships, we must learn to communicate and attune to one another on a heart-to-heart level. Attunement is joining others in their pain and loving them through it. This type of communication cannot happen unless a sense of safety is established and mercy is offered, rather than an insistence upon being "right." The main goals of healthy communication are to gain understanding of the other person's perspective and to graciously care for his or her heart in the process.

1 Peter 3:8-9 is a great exhortation on responding to others appropriately: "Finally, all of you be of one mind, having compassion for one another; love as brothers, be tenderhearted, be courteous; not returning evil for evil or reviling for reviling, but on the contrary blessing, knowing that you were called to this, that you may inherit a blessing."

The following checklist will help you assess whether you are responding to others with blessing:[2]
1. Was I in harmony with him/her?
2. Was I sympathetic?
3. Was I compassionate?
4. Did I demonstrate humility?
5. Did I guard my tongue from returning evil?
6. Did I turn from responding with evil?
7. Did I seek and pursue peace?
8. Did I respond in a gentle way?
9. Did I show respect?

There is a difference between communicating information and connecting heart-to-heart. When we are focused on our own pain and/or agenda, our relational circuits are most likely turned off. Expecting people to lovingly communicate when their relational circuits are off is like expecting them to describe a painting they've never seen with their eyes closed. People cannot respond to (or give) love when they are emotionally locked.

For example, if a father degrades his daughter and responds to her in anger, she will fear him and expect rejection. The fear of being rejected will be transferred to her future husband and will prevent her from opening her heart to him. Consequently, if she perceives her husband is raising his voice, she will emotionally lock up (turning off her relational circuits).The husband, unaware of these issues inside her heart, cannot understand why she responds negatively.[3] Now, his relational circuits will likely turn off, things will escalate, and healthy heart-to-heart communication becomes impossible.

**Courageous Conversation**

An effective tool that can be used to help facilitate healthy communication is called a "Courageous Conversation." It is a communication process that Chris Hogan, a life coach, developed with his wife, Anne, to resolve pressing issues and bring comfort and an increase of trust and feelings of connectedness.

The steps for this process are:
1. Define the problem: Seek an awareness of the "most pressing issue." Once the person sharing his or her feelings expresses what the most pressing issue is, the listener then asks, "In addition to this, is there something else?"
2. Understand the pain: The listener asks questions to draw out the speaker's feelings, such as "How is this affecting you?" and "What will the future be like if nothing changes?"
3. Discuss personal responsibilities: The listener reflects back the speaker's thoughts and feelings – listening, validating, and concluding with: "What do you need?", "What do you see as my responsibility for this issue?", and "What do you see as your responsibility?"
4. Discover preferable future: Resolve needs verbally and with touch: "What does the preferable future look like to you?" and "Would you like to pray together?"
5. Develop a plan: Include "What is the one thing we must not fail to do?"

It is important to note that the person sharing his or her feelings needs to:

1. Speak the truth in love.
2. Provide a safe environment for listening.
3. State facts that support the feelings rather than expressing feelings as facts.
4. Allow the listener to summarize the meaning of the statements being shared.
5. Clarify statements until the listener has understood the message to the speaker's satisfaction.

The role of the listener is to:

1. Listen from the speaker's perspective.
2. Show respect by staying involved in the conversation.
3. Don't complain, explain, or blame.
4. Restate the meaning of the message to the speaker's satisfaction.
5. Gain wisdom and develop understanding to establish a relationship of trust and use knowledge to resolve issues.[4]

## Emotional Comfort through Sharing Our Story with Others

In the book, *Attachments,* Dr. Tim Clinton and Dr. Gary Sibcy discuss the concept of sharing your life story. Recounting portions of our life story with others in a safe and caring environment helps us to gain the freedom to be our true selves without shame. It also helps bring forgotten details out in the open. In doing so, the experiences move from being pictures in our minds to pictures with a story. As our pain is validated, we are better able to gain God's perspective, and the story becomes reframed as God's story. In it, He brings His truth to light and the fragmented pieces come together. God's reframed perspective focuses our understanding of how our spiritual capacity increased, and God's purposes were accomplished through what was gained by the experience. A good example of God's reframing in Scripture is when Joseph was able to testify to his brothers, "You meant evil against me, but God meant it for good" (Gen. 50:20).

There are three important steps involved in order for a person to effectively share parts of his/her story.

Step one – recall the facts:

- How old were you?
- Where were you?
- Who was there?
- How did the situation unfold?
- Were you hurt by the situation? If so, what exactly hurt you?
- What resulted from the hurt?


- Step two – retrace the path of pain:
- How did you feel?
- Were you angry?
- Were you afraid?
- What did you want to happen that didn't?
- How does the incident make you feel now?

Note: One's previous experiences haven't really become memories of the past if he/she still carries the pain in the present. Once painful events are released into words (and feelings are validated), it's possible for soul wounds to be healed because the wounded self is no longer cloaked in denial.

Step three – receive God's reframed perspective (by inviting His comfort into wounded areas):

- How did Jesus feel when the painful event took place?
- What would it have been like if you had known Jesus was there?
- Are there any lies that need to be replaced with truth?

Closing prayer: Thank God for the truth He revealed!

# Chapter 1 Questions

1. Review Dr. Lehman's Relational Circuits Connection Test. Recall a time when you think your relational circuits were turned off. Describe the circumstances and the outcome of the situation.

2. Why it is important to get reconnected with God (turn your relational circuits back on) in order to re-engage your heart?

3. Why are heart-to-heart communication and attunement needed to maintain healthy relationships?

4. What is the listener's role in maintaining healthy communication during a conflict?

5. Why is it important for the speaker to communicate the truth in love (rather than make accusations)?

6.  What is meant by our story being reframed as God's story? Why is this helpful?

7.  What does it mean to carry the pain of past memories in the present? Why is this a problem? Give an example from your life.

8.  What insights have you gained from this chapter? Give an example of how you might apply what you learned to your life.

# Chapter 2

## Our Dark Side – The Carnal Nature

When God created man in the garden, He breathed His **breath of life** into the man's nostrils (Genesis 2:7).[5] Adam's original design was in God's image with complete wholeness in spirit, soul, and body. He and his wife, Eve, experienced unhindered intimacy and communion with their Creator. However, to test their capacity for perfect love and obedience, God placed two trees within the garden of paradise: The Tree of the Knowledge of Good and Evil, and The Tree of Life. He warned them, "but of the tree of the knowledge of good and evil you shall not eat, for **in the day that you eat of it you shall surely die**." – Genesis 2:17

Satan tempted Eve with fruit from The Tree of the Knowledge of Good and Evil because the source of his power (pride and self-exaltation) was rooted in that tree.[6] Ezekiel 28 provides a prophetic picture of when Lucifer (Satan) exalted himself above God and was cast from heaven. When Adam and Eve willfully chose the lust for more knowledge (to make themselves like God) above obedience and trust in God, their human souls became dark. The law of sin and death took over, and their spiritual capacity to know and follow God died (Genesis 3).

In 1 Corinthians 15:56, we learn that "…the strength of sin is the law." This is because it is through the law that we derive our knowledge of good and evil. This knowledge brings death by distracting us from the One who is the source of life – The Tree of Life (Jesus) – causing the focus of our attention to be upon ourselves. Prior to eating fruit from The Tree of the Knowledge of Good and Evil, Adam and Eve had not even noticed their nakedness because their attention was on the Lord and the purposes for which He had created them. However, immediately after eating the forbidden fruit, the good and evil that they then understood forced them to measure themselves by it,[7] thus starting the cycle of shame, denial, and self-preservation.

Adam and Eve had spiritually died, and their primary focus became the natural world around them. Scripture says in I Corinthians 2:14, "But the natural man does not receive the things of the Spirit of God, for they are foolishness to him; nor can he know them, because they are spiritually discerned." As long as we are functioning under bondage to the law of sin (our carnal nature or dark side), we will naturally react to pain and difficulty in a self-preserving carnally minded way. The dark side can be defined as being born with a propensity to sin. It is the selfish part of one's nature that naturally puts its own interests first, and does not have a capacity to truly love. An example would be any action or response that is not motivated by love.

Romans 8:7 states, "Because the carnal (fleshly) mind is enmity against God; for it is not subject to the law of God, nor indeed can be." The Apostle Paul helped explain this dynamic earlier in Romans 7:15-18 and 21, "For what I am doing, I do not understand. For what I will to do, that I do not practice; but what I hate, that I do. If, then, I do what I will not to do, I agree with the law that it is good. But now, it is no longer I who do it, but sin that dwells in me. For I know that in me (that is, in my flesh) nothing good dwells… I find then a law, that evil is present with me, the one who wills to do good."

I will address the solution to this problem of sin later. For now, I want to emphasize that even Christians can live in darkness by consistently turning their hearts and minds away from God and yielding to Satan's temptation. This causes a stronghold of sinful self-will to form in their hearts as James 1:14 explains: "But each one is tempted when he is drawn away by his own desires…" The darkness within only increases because they have given the enemy legal claim in certain areas of their lives.[8] In such cases, the person's heart often becomes divided, or fragmented. James 1:8 and 4:8 refer to some people as being *dipsuchos*, which has been described as meaning two-souled, or split-souled. It is important to recognize that the book of James was written to Christians. These two verses are actually saying that double-minded Christians are two-souled, or split souled, which causes instability in all their ways.[9] Double-mindedness prevents us from experiencing the fullness of God's light and His presence within our hearts.

# Chapter 2 Questions

1. Read Numbers 13:1-3 and 13:30-33. Explain how Caleb's perspective was defined by the Tree of Life and how the 10 spies' perspectives were defined by the Tree of the Knowledge of Good and Evil.

2. Describe a time when you chose to eat from the Tree of the Knowledge of Good and Evil instead of from the Tree of Life.

3. Why were Adam and Eve ashamed when they became aware of their nakedness?

4. What does it mean to be spiritually dead?

5. Why can't the carnal mind be subject to the law of God?

6. Give an example of a person being drawn away by his or her own desires.

7. Using a Bible concordance, find a verse that mentions temptation and explain what it means to you.

8. What does it means to give the enemy legal claim in a certain area of your life?

9. Why is a double-minded Christian unstable in all of his or her ways?

10. Proclaim Romans 8:1-2 over yourself: "There is therefore now no condemnation to those who are in Christ Jesus, who do not walk according to the flesh, but according to the Spirit. For the law of the Spirit of life in Christ Jesus has made me free from the law of sin and death."

11. What insights have you gained from this chapter? Give an example of how you might apply what you learned to your life.

# Chapter 3

## What's Keeping out the Light?

The core of our personality is the person who God created from the foundation of the world.[10] In Psalm 139:13 we read, "For You formed my inward parts…" Ephesians 1:4 says, "…He chose us in Him before the foundation of the world, that we should be holy and without blame before Him in love."

The core personality can be understood as the original or true self. Paul expresses his frustration regarding his own internal struggle between the light and darkness in Romans 7:22-23: "For I delight in the law of God according to the **inward man** (core). But I see another law in my members, warring against the law of my mind, and bringing me into captivity to **the law of sin which is in my members** (dark side)."

In the previous chapter, I briefly described a double-minded person as having a split soul. A helpful analogy of being double-minded and having a split soul is a "duplex", which is a house with a single roof under which two dwelling places exist. A dividing wall in the middle separates one from the other[11].

We are all subject to this duplex symptom that is tied to our Adamic fallen nature. Its dark side is the generations of iniquity passed down from our forefathers. However, the "core" of our personality remains on the "safe" or saved side after salvation, where we can hear the Lord convicting our hearts and wooing us unto Himself.[12]

What keeps a person trapped on the dark side and separated from the Light? We can remain trapped when deprived of the things we should have had in order to develop healthy thinking and living. Trauma resulting from deep childhood wounds can also keep us trapped. The lack of a mature parent or caretaker to provide comfort and nurture in order to help children properly process emotional pain causes them to develop fragmented parts or wounded souls. These parts separate (or fracture) from the core's conscious memory in an effort to dissociate from the pain and live on the dark side of the soul.

When parts separate, a wounded personality can form in which a person's soul gets locked up because of unresolved pain. These wounded parts will often dissociate from the pain by living in a fantasy world within the soul, forming a false self, in order to avoid having to face reality. Often wounded personalities go undetected until the person is going through extreme or prolonged stressful circumstances. A simple example might be times when one overreacts and starts behaving like a child, instead of handling stress like a level-headed adult. Another example might be a person who is normally mild-mannered who shifts into being a control freak whenever he or she feels threatened or fearful. The lie that they are believing might be, "If I stay in control, I won't have to suffer any more pain."

In extreme cases, Hawkins explains that "the core creates wounded personalities to perform certain tasks that the core finds unpleasant. Each of these personalities serves a particular purpose and has its own way of thinking and emotions."[13] Hawkins adds, that "Intolerable psychological conflicts, often based on false beliefs, create a seeming need for denial that leads to dissociation in severely traumatized children."[14] Most likely, "wounded personalities will not go away until they have been led to willingly deal with their issues, repent, and be healed through the mercy and grace of Jesus Christ."[15] In other words, the dissociated part needs to repent and yield to the Lordship of Jesus. A reversal of dissociation involves the integration of false identities into a healthy perception of self, others, and the environment. It is important to note that an individual who is suffering from severe dissociation may be dealing with a psychological disorder called DID (dissociative identity disorder). In such cases, he or she will probably need help from a trained counselor or therapist in order to be emotionally and mentally whole.

Dissociative walls – such as control, fear, pride, and anger – are self-protective mechanisms we hold onto in an effort to keep further pain and disappointment out. The problem is that when we trust in these walls for protection, God's hands become tied, hindering His help and comfort. Therefore, lies are reinforced in our time of need, causing us to feel like God is really not there and that we are on our own, resulting in double-mindedness. In less extreme cases, people are mostly dealing with wounded places in the soul, where they have chosen to believe lies that hold them in darkness. As the Holy Spirit brings conviction of sin, they need to acknowledge the lie, renounce it, and allow the light of God's truth to replace it.

In resolving painful trauma, it is also important to recognize that physiological issues may play a role. For example, there's a part of the brain (hippocampus) that remembers facts but not emotions. When stress levels are high enough, stress hormones hinder this part of the brain from properly functioning. As a result, an accurate time log related to traumatic events does not register in the brain, leaving part of a person bound to the past and reliving those traumatic events as if they were still happening. To resolve this issue, Babette Rothschild, in her book, "Eight Keys to Safe Trauma Recovery," suggests that those traumatized in this way write their own epilogue. It is important to include information from the present in the epilogue that could not have been possible at the time of the trauma. This will help to reinforce that the person survived the trauma and it is now over. For example, a woman who experienced a traumatic event at age ten may include her children in her epilogue since she could not have had kids as a child herself. This will help her brain to realize that she survived the trauma and no longer has to keep reliving the past.

# Chapter 3 Questions

1. Before the foundation of the world, who do you think God created you to be?

2. Describe a time when there has been a war going on in your mind between the light and darkness.

3. Explain the term "dark side" using the duplex analogy.

4. Did you receive emotional comfort and nurture as a child, or were you left to deal with emotional pain on your own? Explain your response.

5. Define a dissociative wall. Provide an example in yourself or someone you know.

6. Describe a wounded personality.

7. Spend a few minutes in prayer and ask the Holy Spirit to reveal any wounded places or self-protective walls in your soul that He desires to heal (use emotional pain words from the appendix at the end of this workbook to help get in touch with your feelings). If the Holy Spirit reveals anything, ask Him if there are any lies you believe that are attached to the pain. If He reveals a specific lie, renounce it in Jesus' name, and ask Him to replace the lie with His truth. Write down whatever He reveals.

8. What insights have you gained from this chapter? Give an example of how you might apply what you learned to your life.

Ministry tool to take down walls:

**Minister:** "God created you to be with His Son, Jesus. You were never supposed to be alone. This wall causes part of you to function independently because lies have kept that part of you from knowing Jesus as the Truth. This _____ (controlling, fearful, prideful, angry, etc.) part must lay down its walls of self-protection and let Jesus come in, in order to heal its wounds and release the fullness of salvation."

**Seeker:** "Jesus, I repent of the lie that says that _____ (control, fear, pride, anger, etc.) is/are more powerful than You and can protect me and keep me safe. I command the spirit(s) of _____ (control, fear, pride, anger, etc.) to be loosed and to go back to where it/they came from. I renounce all double-mindedness in the powerful name of Jesus!"

# Chapter 4

## Toxic Pride

Pride is toxic because it poisons our hearts, causing spiritual sickness. A good analogy of pride can be related to a physical disorder called "Candida", a condition caused by an overgrowth of yeast in the body. When allowed to spread uncontested, this fungal infection produces root-like tentacles that can attach themselves to the intestinal wall, causing dysfunction throughout the body. In a similar manner, pride can "infect" the motives of the heart.

Pride is an exalted view of oneself, expressed in thoughts, attitudes, words, and actions. Examples of pride can be, "look at what I know", "look at what I can do", or "look at what I have." Pride wants to be the best and be in charge. It thinks it knows more than others. When we are prideful, we want to be like the Most High, yet we do not have His character or omnipotence. Pride attempts to steal God's glory. The only thing God encourages us to be proud of is that we know and understand Him (Jeremiah 9:23-24). We are to reject every thought that exalts itself against the knowledge of God (II Corinthians 10:5).[16] Toxic pride, originating from Satan's rebellion and his self-exalting lies (Ezekiel 28), has infected the human race ever since Adam and Eve willfully chose knowledge.

Obvious pride is easy to recognize; it is an exaggerated view of oneself. Hidden pride, however, can be very difficult for people to identify in themselves. It includes a focus on one's inner pain and feelings of rejection that develop into self-pity, resulting in an inability to see anything except one's own needs and feelings.[17] Many unresolved deep wounds result in hidden pride because coping mechanisms of self-comfort and/or self-protection are developed to avoid the pain. Examples of hidden pride include: feeling sorry for ourselves because we're not appreciated, a driving compulsion to have others meet our needs, and focusing on ourselves rather than others.[18] With hidden pride, we are relationally closed and put up walls around our heart to keep others out.

Just as our immune system was designed to fight off infection in our physical bodies, the Holy Spirit desires to fill our hearts and minds with the power of God's love and truth in order to heal and transform us from the inside out. Scripture says that God resists the proud, but gives grace to the humble (James 4:6). If we are not cleansed of pride, it will hinder the spiritual wholeness and emotional comfort that God wants to release into our lives, which ultimately robs us of our true destiny. This cleansing is often very painful because it involves a breaking of our pride and self-deception. God often uses our uncomfortable circumstances to expose (or trigger) those places within us that are not yielded to His Lordship.

The first time God started dealing with the pride in my heart was several years ago. I was at a women's retreat with a group of my friends. At breakfast, I was sharing with one of the ladies how deeply I longed to see God's miraculous power working through my life: healing the sick, casting out demons, and raising the dead. When we entered the meeting hall, worship had already started, so I quietly kneeled down in the back of the room. As soon as I started to focus on the Lord, the Holy Spirit spoke to my heart in a real and personal way. He said, "Pride! I love you too much to fulfill the desires of your heart right now because your pride would destroy you."

This word pierced my heart and provided context for the breaking that I had started going through several months earlier. God's grace has continued to allow me to experience many painful circumstances that have revealed issues in my heart that I would not have been aware of otherwise. Through these trials He is teaching me to be less self-reliant, resist selfish ambition, and be more dependent on Him as my source of strength and righteousness.

Scripture reveals several examples of how God's refining and testing process precedes His blessing. Often, when He speaks a word of promise, He first tests the recipient's heart to ensure the glory goes to the Lord and not to the persons' pride. One biblical example of God's methods for breaking pride and testing the hearts of His children is the story of Job. On the surface, Job's walk appeared blameless. Job 1:8 tells us that God was the initiator of Satan's attack upon Job's life. In the end, Job was made aware of hidden places of pride inside of his nature that he was unaware of when his life was fairly undisturbed. In James 5:11, the Lord reveals that His purpose for the breaking of Job was intended to do him good in the end.

Another example is Abraham (Genesis 12-23), who was chosen by God to be the father of many nations, but Abraham was required to wait many years before the promise was finally fulfilled. During that time of waiting, Abraham's sin of pride and presumption were exposed when he took matters into his own hands. He tried to play God rather than trust God to bring His promise to pass. Other Old Testament examples of God testing the character of His people include Jacob (Genesis 27-32), Joseph (Genesis 37-41), and David (1 Samuel), which tells the story of what David went through prior to becoming king of Israel.

Deuteronomy 8:2-5, is a very good summary of God's breaking and testing process, "And you shall remember that the Lord your God led you all the way these forty years in the wilderness, to humble you and test you, **to know what was in your heart,** whether you would keep His commandments or not. [3] So He humbled you, allowed you to hunger, and fed you with manna which you did not know nor did your fathers know, that He might **make you know** that man shall not live by bread alone; but man lives by every word that proceeds from the mouth of the Lord. [4] Your garments did not wear out on you, nor did your foot swell these forty years. [5] You should know in your heart that as a man chastens his son, so the Lord your God chastens you." Our human nature must be humbled for us to let go of our self-preserving ways and simply follow God's leading with hearts full of faith, feeding our spirit rather than our flesh.

It seems easy to forget how weak and broken most of the apostles were when Jesus initially called them to follow him. Peter is a great example of the Holy Spirit's transforming work within his heart while consistently battling his carnal nature. In Matthew 16:23 Jesus rebuked Peter saying, "Get behind Me, Satan! You are an offense to Me, for you are not mindful of the things of God, but the things of men."

This is a great example of a Christian being split-souled and functioning from the dark side. It's interesting to note that this event was preceded in the same chapter (verse 17) by Jesus commending Peter for his deep comprehension of revelation perceived within his spirit, or inward man, "…'Blessed are you, Simon Bar-Jonah, for flesh and blood has not revealed this to you, but My Father who is in heaven.'"

There are other occasions when Peter's striving, presumption, and pride, were painfully exposed (see Matthew 17:1-5, 26:33-35, and 26:69-75). By the time Peter wrote his first epistle, it is evident in 1 Peter 1:6-7 that he had experienced spiritual transformation in his inner man, "In this you greatly rejoice, though now for a little while, **if need be,** you have been grieved by various trials, that the genuineness of your faith, being much more precious than gold that perishes, though it is tested by fire, may be found to praise, honor, and glory at the revelation of Jesus Christ."

In Psalm 138:6, David wrote, "Though the Lord is on high, yet He regards the lowly; but the proud He knows from afar." Psalm 10:4 says, "The wicked in his proud countenance does not seek God; God is in none of his thoughts." Unresolved pride causes our hearts to be hard and unresponsive to the voice and presence of His Holy Spirit. Therefore, it hinders our relationship with God and others (Proverbs 28:25).

"Scripture teaches us to replace pride with humility."[19] Hession, in his book, *Calvary Road,* agrees, and says, "The Lord Jesus cannot live in us fully and reveal Himself through us until the proud self within us is broken. This simply means that the hard unyielding self, which justifies itself, wants its own way, stands up for its rights, and seeks its own glory, at last bows its head to God's will, admits it's wrong, gives up its own way to Jesus, surrenders its rights, and discards its own glory – that the Lord Jesus might have all and be all. In other words, it is dying to self and self attitudes."[20] "We are not likely to be broken except at the cross of Jesus. The willingness of Jesus to be broken for us is the all-compelling motive in our being broken too."[21]

"Lord, bend that proud and stiff-necked I,
Help me to bow the head and die;
Beholding Him on Calvary,
Who bowed His head for me.
– Author unknown

# Chapter 4 Questions

1. Give an example of a prideful motive of the heart.

2. Why does a prideful attitude steal God's glory?

3. Ask the Holy Spirit to search your heart for hidden areas of pride. Write down anything He shows you.

4. Ask the Holy Spirit if you have any self-comforting or self-protecting coping mechanisms that you are turning to in an effort to avoid facing the pain of certain unresolved issues in your life. Write down anything He reveals.

5. Share about a time in your life where you felt like God was resisting you because of pride in your heart.

6. How would you define self-deception?

7. Describe a situation where God allowed your sinful nature to be triggered through painful circumstances in order to reveal prideful places in your heart that you would not otherwise have recognized.

8. What person in Scripture (other than Jesus) whose character was tested by God do you identify with the most? Why?

9. Ask the Holy Spirit if there are any personal rights that you are holding onto that He wants you to surrender to His Lordship?

10. Pray this closing prayer from your heart: "Lord, I acknowledge attitudes of pride in my heart. I have focused primarily on myself and my rights, interests, needs, desires, and goals. I have neglected to acknowledge and place You first in certain areas of my life. I ask You, Heavenly Father, to open my heart so that I can respond in humility and recognition of who You are. I also ask that You open my heart to love and care for the needs of others around me and that I would esteem them better than myself. I choose to humble myself and acknowledge each area of pride to You. In Jesus' name I pray. Amen."[22]

11. What insights have you gained from this chapter? Give an example of how you might apply what you learned to your life.

# Chapter 5

## Remembering Jesus on the Cross – The Key to Forgiveness

As mentioned previously, the cross is a symbol of death. On Mount Calvary, we remember Jesus, "...who, being in the form of God, did not consider it robbery to be equal with God (not counting equality with God a prize to be grasped and hung onto), but made Himself of no reputation, taking the form of a bondservant, and coming in the likeness of men. ...He humbled Himself and became obedient to the point of death, even the death of the cross." – Philippians 2:6-8.

Jesus was perfectly innocent, yet, "We see Him willing to have no rights of His own, willing to let men revile Him and not revile again, willing to let men tread on Him and not retaliate or defend Himself. Above all, we see Him broken as He goes to Calvary to become men's scapegoat by bearing their sins in His own body on the Tree."[23]

When recently talking with a friend, we both recognized for the first time that the word "give" is right in the middle of the word, for-give-ness. Redemption is a **gift from the heart of Jesus** to those who will, by faith, exchange their old life of sin (death to self) for His (spiritual life). "But dying to self is not a thing we do once and for all. There may be an initial dying when God first shows us these things, but ever after it will be a continual dying, for only so can the Lord Jesus be revealed constantly through us (2 Corinthians 4:10 and Matthew 16:24-25). All day long the choice will be before us in a thousand ways... It will mean a constant yielding to those around us, for our yieldedness to God is measured by our yieldedness to man."[24]

In the parable of the unmerciful servant (Matthew 18:23-35), Jesus paints a powerful picture of the vastness of His gift of forgiveness to us and how necessary it is for us to also give that same gift of forgiveness, **from our hearts**, to those who have sinned against us. Just as God cancelled our debt against Him, which we could never repay, He requires us to cancel the debt that we feel others owe to us.

The Matthew 18 passage (verse 34) also describes how people are left imprisoned and emotionally tortured whenever they will not forgive their fellow servants. Unforgiveness is one of the main blocks and hindrances to spiritual wholeness and emotional comfort. Matthew 6:14-15 says, "For if you forgive men their trespasses, your heavenly Father will also forgive you. But if you do not forgive men their trespasses, neither will your Father forgive your trespasses."

People often imagine that dying to self and letting go of offense will make them miserable, but just the opposite is true. It is the refusal to die to self and forgive that makes one miserable. The more we know of death with Him, the more we shall know of the wholeness of His life in us, and the more we will have real peace and joy.[25]

"In order to better understand the power of the cross, we must remember that when Jesus chose the cross and took it up and carried it and finally died on it, He did this as the second Adam... By dying on the cross as Mediator, He obtained the life of glory."[26] As believers, we are released from sin's bondage and are united to Him. Therefore, we can start to live by the power of His holy nature within our hearts: "I have been crucified with Christ; it is no longer I who live, but Christ lives in me; and the life which I now live in the flesh I live by faith in the Son of God, who loved me and gave Himself for me." – Galatians 2:20. Andrew Murray tells us, "We have the power in all things and at all times to choose the cross in spite of the 'old man' and the world, to choose the cross and to let it do its work."[27] He also encourages us by saying, "It is only when we rightly understand and receive into our hearts the love of which the cross speaks that we can experience its full power and blessing."[28]

> Oh, to be saved from myself, dear Lord,
> Oh, to be lost in Thee,
> Oh, that it be no more I,
> But Christ that lives in me.
> – Author unknown

# Chapter 5 Questions

1. Explain why forgiveness is a gift.

2. Why do you think that the degree to which we are yielded to God is measured by how yielded we are to man?

3. Imagine your creditor canceling the largest debt you've ever owed. Describe how that thought makes you feel.

4. Explain a time when you (or someone you know) were emotionally tormented because of refusing to forgive.

5. What does it mean to be crucified with Christ?

6. What does it mean to live by faith in the Son of God? Give an example of a time when you had to step out in faith and trust God.

7. Describe a time when you chose to die to yourself and embrace the cross.

8. Make a list of people who have hurt you in the past. Next to each name, describe how he/she hurt you and the emotional pain this caused. Pray and ask the Holy Spirit for the grace to forgive any offense you are still holding. Then pray specifically for each one, "Lord, I choose to forgive _____ (name of individual) for _____ (state the offense), causing me to feel _____ (use emotional pain words – see appendix at the end of the book). [I willingly choose to cancel this debt.]* I ask You, Lord Jesus, to take back the ground I gave to the enemy through my bitterness, and I yield that ground to Your control."[29]

* Bracketed content inserted by author.

# Chapter 6

## Anxiety – Static That Prevents Hearing

If static is present while listening to a radio, it makes it almost impossible to properly hear what is being broadcast. In the same way, anxious thoughts in the soul make it very difficult to hear the Lord's still small voice speaking to our spirit. Feelings of insecurity are usually the root of anxiety. *not feeling secure or safe*

I remember as a child lying on my bed at night shaking from the inside out, fearing what my father was going to do next. Although he never physically abused me, he was severely mentally ill and emotionally unstable. Due to these issues, I was not able to trust him to properly care for my needs. Therefore, a stronghold of anxiety formed in my heart. It has taken many years for God to dismantle this stronghold and bring comfort and rest to that broken part of my soul.

Attachment pain occurs when people feel unloved and have limited emotional connection to the primary people who are supposed to love them. This type of pain is the natural result of feeling a loss of connection, causing anxiety. Only God's love can fill the void created by this type of loss. There are specific moments when God enlightened my understanding regarding special ways He provided for my needs when my earthly father was not able to be there for me. I personally connect with Psalm 94:19, "In the multitude of my anxieties within me, Your comforts delight my soul."

Many years ago, during my quiet times with God, I would pray David's prayer from Psalm 139:23-24, "Search me, O God, and know my heart; try me, and know my anxieties; and see if there is any wicked way in me, and lead me in the way everlasting."

When our hearts are anxious, it means that we are not trusting God to meet our needs. In Luke 12:29, Jesus exhorted His disciples by saying, "And do not seek what you should eat or what you should drink, nor have an anxious mind." Putting our trust in God and His truth is the foundation of our faith and necessary for spiritual wholeness and emotional healing to manifest in our lives.

For some of us, anxiety is such a core part of our personality that we may not recognize we are anxious. Some examples of common symptoms of anxiety include:

- Physical – heart racing, tense muscles, facial twitches, dry mouth, difficulty swallowing, sweating, nervous stomach, and shaking
- Emotional – racing, negative, and/or fearful thoughts; restlessness
- Behavioral – tendency toward food/other addictions, inability to eat, irritability, compulsive control, and difficulty sleeping

An important skill to develop is the ability to self quiet (soothe myself) in the midst of this kind of distress as well as from high levels of excitement. As we begin to physically relax, we can then quiet our hearts and tune in to God to receive His peace. (In the next chapter, we will go into more detail on finding God's rest.) In this chapter, the specific focus is on quieting anxiety. This is addressed well in some training materials from a ministry called Thrive. In these materials, soothe myself/simple quiet (one of 19 relational brain skills) involves the intentional "lowering (of) my own energy level so I can rest after both joyful (feelings of excitement) and upsetting emotions, as I need to and on my own… This self-soothing capacity is the strongest predictor of good mental health for the lifetime." It is described in the Thrive materials as the "release-on-demand of serotonin (a calming brain chemical)… to quiet both positive and distressing emotional states."[30]

Once we recognize we are feeling anxious, as difficult as it is, we can make the choice to quiet ourselves. How best to do so is different for each individual, so it is important to try different approaches and learn what works. Some common ways to self-quiet include:

- Become aware of your breathing and take intentional, slow deep breaths.
- Take a relaxing bath
- Sit with your feet up outside on a sunny day
- Take a casual walk
- Listening or playing music

- Playing with a child or favorite pet
- Laughter

Try some of these activities and pay attention to how they make you feel. With successful self quiet, you should notice slower breathing and less tense muscles. Once you are able to come to a place of physical rest, you should be better able to quiet your heart and tune in to hearing God.

If you are noticing some of the symptoms of anxiety, be sure to pray the recommended prayer in question 7 at the end of this chapter.

# Chapter 6 Questions

1. Remember a time when you turned on a radio and tried listening when there was static. Were you able to effectively hear the music or program that was playing? Describe a time when you felt you couldn't hear God because of the static of anxiety in your soul.

2. What are some areas of insecurity in your life that cause you to feel anxious? Can you trace them to times in your childhood when your needs were not met?

Dramatic or emotionally overwhelming people
unmanageability of emotions or thoughts
Doubting my ability to hear from or perceive God.
Doubting the security of God's constant presence.
fear of my mental state (feeling out of control of my own sanity)

3. Take time to pray David's prayer in Psalm 139:23-24, "Search me, O God, and know my heart; try me, and know my anxieties; and see if there is any wicked way in me, and lead me in the way everlasting." Write down whatever He reveals.

4. Ask the Holy Spirit to show you whether there is anything that may be keeping you from fully trusting Him. Write down what He says.

5. Pray and invite the Lord's comforts to delight your soul (Psalm 94:19). Write down your experience.

6. Try some of the suggested approaches to self-quieting mentioned at the end of this chapter. Pay attention to signs of your body relaxing (breathing, tense muscles, etc.). Record your experiences. Identify at least one way you found to be effective.

7. If you sense that you may have a stronghold of fear (anxiety) in your heart, pray the following prayer: "Heavenly Father, I choose to lay down the self-protective wall of fear that I have placed around my heart. Jesus, come in to heal my wounds and release the fullness of Your salvation. For You have not given me a spirit of fear, but of power, love, and a sound mind (2 Timothy 1:7). In the name of Jesus and by the authority of His shed blood, I renounce the spirit of fear and its manifestations and fruit. I repent for my lack of trusting, doubt, worry, unbelief, and anxiety. In the name of Jesus, I break the power of panic attacks, torment, horror, terror, nightmares, fear of the dark, and fear of death! I repent of and renounce a hermit and reclusive spirit and all forms of introversion. I repent of and renounce an alone spirit. I repent of and renounce the fear of man and the fear of relationships, abuse, rejection, and abandonment. I repent of and renounce extreme forms of extroversion and perfectionism and the fear of authority, saying no, and failure. I repent of and renounce the fear of sickness, the fear of not being good enough, and all other phobias. I repent of and renounce any obsession with or addiction to food. I repent and renounce an unhealthy fear of God, and, in the name of Jesus, I break the power of any familiar spirits of fear that have been passed down through my family line. Holy Spirit, what do you have for me to replace fear and anxiety?"

Explain what you were sensing after you prayed this prayer.

59

# Chapter 7

## Finding the Spirit Within – Our Source of Comfort

Ephesians 3:16-19 says, "...that He would grant you, according to the riches of His glory, to be strengthened with might through **His Spirit in the inner man**, that **Christ may dwell in your hearts** through faith, that you being rooted and grounded in love, may be able to comprehend with all the saints what is the width and length and depth and height – **to know the love of Christ which passes knowledge**; that you may be filled with all the fullness of God." This passage gives us a key to finding His Spirit within our inner man. While our mind, which is part of our soul, may know about the love of God, it is only through our heart that we may actually comprehend, or intuitively sense, the love of God. It is the personal experience of deeply encountering the Presence of God within our heart that gives us comfort.

In God's original design, the soul of man functioned in full submission to his human spirit, which was in perfect harmony with God's Spirit. However, after the fall, man's inner nature or heart became soul dominant and his spirit died (Genesis 2:17 and Genesis 3), becoming lost within the soul. At salvation, God's Spirit comes and dwells within our spirit (1 Corinthians 6:19-20 and 2 Corinthians 13:5).

Hebrews 4:12 says, "For the word of God is living and powerful, and sharper than any two-edged sword, piercing even to the division of the soul and spirit, and of joints and marrow, and is a discerner of the thoughts and intents of the heart." Earlier in this same chapter (verses 1-11), the writer of Hebrews was teaching about the importance of entering into God's rest through faith (spiritually), rather than hardening our hearts in soulish striving and unbelief.

Entering into God's rest can also be referred to as the quieting of the soul in order to perceive God's Spirit within our heart. "Prayer (or communing with His Spirit) is standing in the presence of God with the mind in the heart; that is, at the point of our being where there are no divisions or distinctions and where we are totally one. There God's Spirit dwells and there the great encounter takes place. There, heart speaks to heart, because there we stand before the face of the Lord, all seeing, within us."[31] This is a picture of inner healing being released. "By its very nature such prayer transforms our entire being into Christ precisely because it opens the eyes of our soul to the truth of ourselves as well as the truth of God (Colossians 3:10). In our heart, we come to see ourselves as sinners embraced by the mercy of God."[32] This produces comfort, and our hearts are touched with healing and made whole.

As mentioned in previous chapters, there are many hindrances to finding God as our authentic source of comfort. In an effort to regulate our negative emotions, we can become trapped into attaching to areas of false comfort. The lie believed might be, "If I can feel good physically or find fulfillment outside of myself, then I will be okay." This can manifest in various commonly recognized addictive behaviors, such as overeating, drugs and alcohol, excessive busyness, gambling, and overly indulgent shopping and entertainment. Less obvious forms of false comfort are habitual self-pity and a victim mentality, where we shift our responsibility onto others through blame and false accusations. Finally, sex addictions, including masturbation and pornography, are common sources of false comfort that are often not addressed because of the stigma of shame. All of these behaviors are pseudo-comforts that bring guilt and shame and prevent us from finding God as our true source of comfort. To address these issues, it is important to find true joy and comfort in a safe community where you can be honest, accountable, and begin the journey of laying down counterfeit comforts in exchange for God's comfort.

After false comforts are repented of, the primary way to find inward and lasting comfort is by quieting the soul and finding the Holy Spirit within, which takes discipline and practice. Back in the early eighties, Mark and Patti Virkler developed a study guide called, Communion with God. In one of the chapters about becoming still, they wrote, "Often we miss the importance of quieting ourselves as we approach God. Our lives are such a rush; we just run up to God, blurt out our prayers, and rush away again. I am convinced that we will never enter the realm of the Spirit that way… In order for our inner man to commune with God we must first remove external distractions, where we can center down into our hearts… Second, we must learn to quiet our inner being where all the voices within us are calling for our attention… Write down anything that comes to your mind that can be taken care of later, and quiet your inner members by focusing them on Jesus (perceiving His presence). Next, become tuned into the inner cry of your heart, and repeat it over and over; this may also include a spontaneous song. At this point, you may find tension within your body that needs to be released. Learn to consciously relax the parts of your body that are tense… Check your breathing and use it to help you relax… It can be helpful to imagine you are breathing in the pure Spirit of Christ and breathing out the contaminated spirit of self… In becoming still, don't 'try' to do anything. Simply get in touch with the Divine Lover and center in on this moment of time, experiencing Him in it. Becoming still cannot be hurried or forced. Rather, it must be allowed to happen. At a point in your stillness, God takes over and you sense His active flow within you. His spontaneous images begin to flow with life of their own. His voice begins speaking, giving you wisdom and strength. You find that you are 'in the Spirit' (Revelation 1:10)."[33]

# Chapter 7 Questions

1. Explain the difference between your inner and outward man. Why is it important for your inner man to be strengthened?

2. Describe a time when Father God revealed the love of Christ to you in a real and personal way.

3. What does it mean to be filled with the fullness of God?

4. What do you think it means for God's word to divide the soul from the spirit?

5. Explain a time when you experienced God's rest.

6. Why do you think striving and unbelief keep our hearts from knowing God's rest?

7. Describe a time when you were feeling emotionally overwhelmed and God brought His comfort to your soul.

8. Ask the Holy Spirit to search your heart to reveal any areas of false comfort. Write down what He shows you. (Note, if the Holy Spirit revealed any areas of false comfort, finding a safe community where you can be honest and accountable will be important for your process of healing and freedom.)

9. Why do you think that many Christians keep themselves overly busy and distracted? What are some external distractions in your life?

10. Follow the instructions from the "Communion with God" description from this chapter. Write down your experience and whatever God reveals to you while you are encountering His Spirit within you.

11. What insights have you gained from this chapter? Give an example of how you might apply what you learned to your life.

**Ministry Tool:**

The following tool helps others access God's comfort through the use of visual images.

An effective way that God can bring His comfort to our emotions is through visual imagery. Engaging the imagination while dialoging with the Holy Spirit makes use of both the right (emotions) and left (logic) hemispheres of the brain. When our brain is fully engaged, old distorted images can be renewed through an inner experiential understanding of truth. In other words, the use of our imagination, while guided by the Holy Spirit, helps us picture life the way God sees it. These pictures that God paints within our hearts are critical to how we emotionally perceive life and others.

Christ's frequent use of parables is a good example of this principle. While teaching in parables, Jesus strategically engaged His listeners' imaginations, giving them a new way of perceiving their inner life. David Eckman, in his book, *Becoming Who God Intended,* gives an example of this from the parable in Matthew 6:26-30. He writes, "In the face of those anxieties (fear about lack of food and clothing), Jesus painted a picture within their imaginations of the world as God the Father and He really saw it. *'Look at the birds of the air, that they do not sow, neither do they reap, nor gather into barns, and your heavenly Father feeds them...And why are you anxious about clothing? Observe how the lilies of the field grow...even Solomon in all of his glory did not clothe himself like one of these...'* Placing the picture of well-taken-care-of birds and lilies in His audience's imaginations, Jesus described to them what reality was really like. God takes care of lowly animals and plants – will He not also take care of humans, who are more significant than the planet itself? He was painting a picture with their imaginations that would give them the new world they could enter by faith in the Father's provision. The beauty of the imagination is that when we focus on the pictures, we enter the world of the pictures, and the emotions of our hearts rise to match the pictures. We can exist emotionally within that world and feel its security and care."

It's important to note that use of mental pictures is just one of many ministry tools. God speaks to each of us in a variety of ways. Some readily see vivid pictures with their mind's-eye, and mental pictures work well for them. For others, God may use an illustration in the natural. An example would be a woman with deep father wounds who is driving down the road and sees a loving father helping his young daughter learn how to ride her bike. At the time the woman sees this picture with her natural eye, she is deeply impacted by how Father God is standing by her side, loving and caring for her. In addition to visual images, God may also choose to communicate through a feeling or by speaking a Scripture or truth that brings comfort.

Ministry using visual images:

**Minister:** "God gave you an imagination. Are you willing to ask His Holy Spirit to come and speak to you there?"

*If the seeker agrees, minister leads the seeker in the following prayer:*

**Seeker:** "Father God, I bind the enemy's influence within my imagination, in the name of Jesus, so that I might clearly hear from You. Holy Spirit, come, cleanse, fill, and sanctify my imagination with Your holy presence. Jesus, please paint me a picture of what you want to show me right now."

**Minister:** "Holy Spirit, is there a key memory that you want to reveal?"

*If the seeker reports a memory, minister leads the seeker in the following question:*

**Seeker:** "Jesus, could You draw me a picture of how that painful event damaged my heart?"

**Minister:** "Father God, I ask You to hold this wounded place in his/her heart and release Your truth and comfort."

# Chapter 8

## Truth in the Inward Parts – Maturity Versus Immaturity

Getting stuck in one or more of the negative emotions of sadness, anger, fear, disgust, shame, and hopeless despair is generally the result of faulty belief systems (or lies within the soul) that stem from unresolved pain or trauma from the past. When our soul is overwhelmed by one or more of these six major emotions, our relational circuits are generally shut down toward God, others, and even our own hearts, and our heart becomes locked.

Our hearts become locked when we erect walls of self-protection around them as a self-defense mechanism, attempting to suppress or keep out further pain. For example, stress, trauma, and inadequate parenting can cause children to feel anxious about how to get what they need, and an anxious core forms instead of a core of trust. Children often respond to this type of pain by developing a system of lies, for example: "I'm on my own, so I'll have to meet my own needs," "If I'm good, I will avoid criticism, and things will be peaceful," or "I must cover my fears by either fighting back or detaching and complying."[34]

As in the Garden of Eden (see Genesis 3:1-5), Satan continues to tempt mankind to question God's goodness. These questions often form earlier in life, when significant caretakers are absent or not available to provide proper nurture and guidance through life's changes and difficulties. If left unresolved, secure attachments do not properly develop, and the child's emotional needs for basic trust are impaired. Consequently, to cope with unmet needs, they slip into denial (in an effort to dissociate) or turn to addictions to find comfort and relief from the pain. Hawkins notes that "Dissociation is held in place by wrong beliefs which seemingly necessitate the need to separate from and deny major portions of the person's history, causing them to live out of a fear-based false identity rather than who they really are at a heart level."[35]

71

Our image of God is often filtered through our view of our parents. People with significant mother and father wounds often struggle with immature behaviors and child-like reactions in their adult lives. A good example of this type of immature behavior is when Paul was addressing the church at Corinth in I Corinthians 3:1-3, "And I, brethren, could not speak to you as to spiritual people, but as to carnal, as to **babes** in Christ. I fed you with milk and not with solid food; for until now you were not able to receive it, and even now you are still not able; for you are still carnal. For where there are envy, strife, and divisions among you, are you not carnal and behaving like mere men?"

Maturity, however, is evidenced in, "a growing ability to act like our true self, while handling increasing levels of complexity, chaos, confusion, and conflict, thus being able to suffer well, without being traumatized. When this capacity is sufficient, we are able to remain relational (and level-headed), even through disagreements and persecution (or other forms of distress)."[36] Just as children mature when they are taught age-appropriate skills and begin to do them, both spiritual and emotional maturity occurs as we learn to walk out God's truths in our lives.

As parents, we do not have to teach our children to sin. They come into the world that way naturally. This inborn sin nature within all of us represents our immature self. In reality, we will remain immature in certain areas until self-discipline is established, and ultimately, until God's love and truth transform us from the inside out. An example of this dynamic might be an adult who shifts into behaving like a child whenever denied something he or she really desires. It is important to understand that, if self-discipline is the only thing keeping us from sin, when placed in the right uncomfortable circumstances, our immature "true colors" will surely come out. As Christians, we can be assured that our Heavenly Father will purposely allow us to encounter various trials in order for us to recognize our need to grow up.

Denial is one of the biggest hindrances to receiving truth and growing in maturity. It keeps our heart locked and, therefore, unable to reach full maturity. Denial is usually rooted in fear, guilt, or shame. The meaning of the word denial is, "to contradict, reject, deny, or refuse." Whenever we willfully choose to reject the truth, certain places (or parts) of our hearts become fertile soil for the lies of the enemy. These lies then take root and grow into strongholds of deception and, unless repented of, hinder us from becoming who God intended us to be. Denial causes our false self to rule and our true self to be suppressed (Colossians 3:9-10), hindering spiritual wholeness and emotional maturity.

For example, when King David fell into sin, he tried to hide his sin and became miserable, illustrating that we can run from God's truth, but we can't hide. In the beginning of that season of David's life, his sin was confronted by the prophet Nathan. Before Nathan confronted him, David's conflicted thinking may have been along the lines of, "I am a moral person" (denial) versus "I have done immoral and evil things" (conviction of truth). After the confrontation, David repented and returned to a place of truthfulness or wholeness in his heart.

David wrote two psalms about this experience. In Psalm 32, he expresses the conflict that goes on within our souls when we are in denial (verses 1-5): "Blessed is he whose transgression is forgiven, whose sin is covered. Blessed is the man to whom the Lord does not impute iniquity, and in whose spirit there is no deceit. When I kept silent, my bones grew old through my groaning all the day long. For day and night Your hand was heavy upon me; my vitality was turned into the drought of summer. I acknowledged my sin to You, and my iniquity I have not hidden. I said, 'I will confess my transgressions to the Lord,' and You forgave the iniquity of my sin." In Psalm 51:6, David shows that he understands the value of having a clean heart: "Behold, You desire truth in the **inward parts**, and in the hidden part You will make me to know wisdom."

One symptom of denial in a person's heart is harsh judgments against others. Jesus warned against this when He said not to judge one another in Matthew 7:1-5: "Do not judge, or you too will be judged. For in the same way you judge others, you will be judged, and with the measure you use, it will be measured to you. "Why do you look at the speck of sawdust in your brother's eye and pay no attention to the plank in your own eye? How can you say to your brother, 'Let me take the speck out of your eye,' when all the time there is a plank (of judgment because of denial) in your own eye? You

73

hypocrite, first take the plank out of your own eye, and then you will see clearly to remove the speck from your brother's eye."

Another common symptom is a tendency toward frequent shifts into dissociation, which is when part of a person splits off into a state of denial in order to escape from pain or trauma. Denial is the glue that holds dissociation in place. When truth is acknowledged and embraced, then denial is no longer needed and neither is dissociation.[37]

In addition, blame-shifting is a form of denial and a self-defense mechanism to get the focus off of ourselves and onto someone else. Referring back to the example in the Garden of Eden, when God confronted Adam with his sin, Adam blamed Eve. When God confronted Eve, she blamed the serpent (Genesis 3:12-13). In marriage counseling, I have found that blame-shifting and denial – expressed by one spouse coming with the expectation of "fixing" the other without wanting to change themselves – is one of the biggest hindrances to making relational progress.

A perfect example of not taking responsibility for our own actions (denial) is Cain's response to God's questioning him about Abel. Cain had just killed his own brother, yet responded by saying, "Am I my brother's keeper?" (Genesis 4:9)

If you are recognizing tendencies toward denial in yourself, you may want to pray the recommended prayer in question 12 at the end of this chapter.

# Chapter 8 Questions

1. Describe a time when you felt stuck in a state of sadness, anger, fear, disgust, shame, or hopeless despair. Ask the Holy Spirit what faulty belief system (or lies) may have caused you to remain trapped in any of these major negative emotions. Write down whatever He shows you.

2. Explain a situation when you put up a wall as a self-defense mechanism in an effort to keep others (including God) out.

3. Was a core of trust properly formed within you as a child, or do you tend to have an anxious core?

4. Ask the Holy Spirit if any lies formed within your heart during childhood as a response to pain. Write down what He reveals.

5. Identify who your significant caretakers were while you were growing up. Did they provide proper nurture and guidance during your life's changes and difficulties? Explain.

6. Describe your present unmet needs. Take time to express those unmet needs to God and ask Him what His perspective is about them. Write down His response.

7. What addictions have you struggled with in an effort to dissociate from pain?

8. Explain whether you've ever lived out of a fear-based identity rather than from who you are at a heart level.

9. Think of how you generally react to difficulty. Are there areas in your adult life where your responses are immature?

10. Read Matthew 21:12-13, 21:23-27, 26:36-68, and 27:11-14. Describe how Jesus modeled a mature response to persecution and stress.

11. How can we act like our true self while experiencing stress and difficulty?

12. Why is denial one of the biggest hindrances to receiving truth and growing in maturity? Give an example from your own life of a time when you were in denial.

13. If the Holy Spirit highlighted some issues of denial or immaturity, pray the following: "Father God, I see that I am trapped in negative emotions and immature responses. Search my heart and show me where I'm in denial, locked up, and unable to live from my true heart. I renounce the lies that You've shown me of _____ (name the lies). In the name of Jesus, I lay down my self-protective walls of _____ (name the walls) that are keeping my heart from connecting with Your Holy Spirit and others. I repent of turning to the addictions of _____ (name them) that I have used to escape pain rather than receiving the comfort of your truth. I forgive my former caretakers _____ (names) for not meeting my needs. Help my heart to align with your perspective about my true needs verses my wants. I ask that you would minister to my heart and establish a core of trust to redeem me from an anxious and insecure identity. Lord, what would you like to give me in exchange for all of these things? (Pause and listen for His response.) In Jesus' name I pray, amen."

Write down what God shows you.

my perfectionism is self-centered.
i realize how I fell short, Then get in a swirl of beating myself up, which keeps my eyes off of You & keeps me from moving forward.

courage admitting That I don't have The means within me to do it & reaching out my hand to grab Yours.

Return "without You I can do no better"

Holy Spirit, will You show me The lies That fuel The stronghold of shame I feel when i fall short or fail?

14. What insights have you gained from this chapter? Give an example of how you might apply what you learned to your life.

# Chapter 9

# We Are Who Our Heavenly Father Says We Are!

Rejection, especially from those we love, can really cut through our hearts like a knife. When these types of wounds remain unhealed, a spirit of rejection can oppress and take over a person's life. At that point, everything we see and experience is filtered through a distorted grid. Most people with this type of oppression can't receive God's love because they often believe that He has rejected them as well. Most commonly, a spirit of rejection is the result of an unhealthy fear of man. Proverbs 29:25 says, "The fear of man brings a snare (of the enemy), but whoever trusts in the Lord shall be safe."

In the introduction, I briefly mentioned an extremely painful situation that I had to face. I was devastated by the harsh judgments that people had made against me. One morning, I looked in the mirror and asked the Lord to tell me what He thought about me. Later that day, I opened my Bible, and my eyes were immediately drawn to 1 Peter 2:4, "...rejected indeed by men, but chosen by God and precious." My Heavenly Father was so faithful to answer the question that I had asked Him earlier that day. He used those words from Scripture to deeply comfort my heart.

Fathers are designed by God to speak identity into their children. However, like my dad, many fathers are so bound by their own emotional brokenness that they cannot properly nurture their own children. Even if an earthly father does a decent job of forming healthy identities in his children, most children still face painful rejection throughout their lives from various friendships and acquaintances. In Revelation 12:10, the Bible calls Satan, "the accuser of our brethren." He thrives on wounding and damaging our hearts through others' careless words and sometimes overt meanness.

If anyone could have been fatally wounded by rejection, it was David. For many years, he was hunted like an animal by King Saul (1 Samuel 19-27). David also experienced significant rejection at various times by his own family members. However, by the time he wrote Psalm 139, he seemed to have a solid understanding of who God had created him to be (verses 13, 14, 17, and 18), "For You formed my inward parts; You covered me in my mother's womb. I will praise You, for **I am fearfully and wonderfully made**. Marvelous are Your works**, and that my soul knows very well**... How precious also are Your thoughts to me, O God! How great is the sum of them! If I should count them, they would be more in number than the sand; when I awake, I am still with You." In 1 Samuel 13:14, God referred to David's identity as, "a man after God's own heart." That is how God saw David, and, to David, it was all that mattered. The opinions of others can shift like the wind, but what God thinks or says about us lasts for eternity.

Jesus is our perfect example of how to live victoriously out of our true identity rather than the opinions of man. At the time of his baptism (Matthew 3:16-17): "... heaven was opened, and he saw the Spirit of God descending like a dove and alighting on him. And a voice from heaven said, 'This is my Son, whom I love; with him I am well pleased.'" Jesus was able to overcome every trial and accusation against His identity by remaining anchored in the truth of who the Father said He was:

- Jesus went into the wilderness immediately after His baptism; with the words of His Father in His heart, He was able to overcome Satan's temptations to find His identity in the things the world had to offer (Luke 4:1-13)
- While in great agony in the Garden of Gethsemane, Jesus was able to submit to the will of His Father, knowing that dying on the cross was his life's destiny (Luke 22:42-44)
- While suffering on the cross, His very own people were making cruel accusations and rejecting Him; still, He was able to say, "Father, forgive them for they know not what they do" (Luke 23:34)

Similar to how Jesus lived out of knowing who His Heavenly Father said He was, understanding our true identity has to come from within. If you are struggling with knowing your true identity and easily impacted by the opinions of others, you may want to make the declarations in question 6 and pray the recommended prayer in question 7 at the end of this chapter.

# Chapter 9 Questions

1. Describe a time when the sting of rejection cut through your heart like a knife.

2. How would you define the "fear of man?"

3.  Why do you think the fear of man causes a snare of the enemy in our lives?

4.  What kind of identity did your earthly father form in your heart?

5.  Why does Satan like to bring accusations against us before God?

6. Take a moment to meditate on these Scriptures: Psalm 45:10-11, Psalm 139:1-18, Song of Solomon 4:7, Romans 8:32-39, 1 Corinthians 1:25-31, Hebrews 13:5-6, and 1 John 4:16-19. Then declare out loud the following statements that define who your Heavenly Father says you are:

   • "I am a worthwhile person whether others realize it or not. God's opinion of my value is what is true and what matters."
   • "God's view of success is different from man's view."
   • "I don't need others' approval or love to feel secure and lovable."
   • "Some people can't like or love me because of their own personal problems."
   • "Since I am always loved by God, I do not need to be overly concerned about the approval or disapproval of others."
   • "God accepts and loves me, although He does not always approve of everything I do."

7. If you have struggled in any way with a spirit of rejection, consider repeating the following prayer by John Regier (modified to address rejection): "Heavenly Father, I ask You to heal all the areas of my heart that were damaged by rejection. I give myself to You and ask You to free me from the emotional barrier caused by the fear of rejection in my life. I desire that my heart be totally free to respond openly and not be locked to others or to You as a result of my past mistreatment. I want to experience Your peace and comfort in each area of my heart that has been damaged through abuse. I want to be free to love and to respond in love under Your creative plan. In Jesus' name I pray. Amen."[38]

8. What insights have you gained from this chapter? Give an example of how you might apply what you learned to your life.

# Chapter 10

## Closing Comments and Inner Healing Resources

In summary, spiritual wholeness and emotional comfort are necessary components for true and lasting inner healing to occur. Without spiritual wholeness, we are disconnected from the life and power of God. Looking to Jesus and His atoning work on the cross releases us from the power of sin and its resulting pain and consequences.

In Christ, by the indwelling of His Spirit, God creates in us a new nature – an awakened spirit – that softens our heart toward God (2 Corinthians 5:17, Ezekiel 36:26). Our enemy, Satan, will do everything he can to keep us bound to the past and reacting from our old carnal nature. Jesus modeled and clearly gave His disciples the remedy to Satan's temptation in Luke 9:23-24: "…If anyone desires to come after Me, let him deny himself, and take up his cross daily, and follow Me. For whoever desires to save his life will lose it, but whoever loses his life for My sake will save it." As we deny ourselves and yield daily to His Holy Spirit's presence within us, He will speak His truth to our heart and comfort our soul. Isaiah 26:3 says, "You will keep him in perfect peace, **whose mind is stayed on You**, because he trusts in You."

In Matthew 22:37-40, Jesus was asked what the greatest commandment was and He answered by saying, "You shall love the Lord your God with all your heart, with all your soul, and with all your mind. This is the first and great commandment. And the second is like it: you shall love your neighbor as yourself…" Maintaining healthy relationships with God and others is a clear sign that we are spiritually whole. We can maintain emotional comfort in our relationships with one another by being intentional about staying connected to the Holy Spirit and caring for the hearts of those that God has placed in our lives through healthy communication.

There are times when we ourselves, and those we know, are spiritually and emotionally oppressed and, therefore, not able to process pain in a healthy way. This is when the ministry of inner healing can be very helpful. In the past several years, I have been privileged to minister with others to help bring healing to wounded hearts.

The following are some resources I've found helpful for training and use in ministry:

1. John and Paula Sanford founded the Elijah House Ministry several years ago. They have a DVD training school that covers a range of topics, including performance orientation, forgiveness, inner vows, bitter-root judgments and expectancy, burden bearing, and the slumbering spirit.

2. Another helpful DVD training resource is "Theophostics" by Ed Smith. Mr. Smith has an excellent prayer ministry model of asking the Holy Spirit questions that help people get in touch with painful memories and inviting the Holy Spirit to expose lies and bring truth to wounded places of their hearts.

3. Dr. Karl Lehman's "Immanuel Process" is similar to Theophostics. The main difference with this approach is that the person receiving ministry is encouraged to focus on perceiving the Holy Spirit's presence and finding Jesus in a memory.

4. Thrive Training, Chris and Jen Coursey, www.thrivetoday.org. "Thrive exists to restore the missing relational brain skills in families, leaders and churches that keep loving people from thriving. We can only pass on to our children and future generations the abilities we have received and refined. By combining brain science with God's way of life and systematic training, we are changing our generation."

# Chapter 10 Questions

1. Why are spiritual wholeness and emotional comfort necessary components for true and lasting inner healing to occur?

2. On a personal level, what does the cross of Christ mean to you?

3. Explain what it means to keep your mind stayed on the Lord.

4. What does it mean to love God with all your heart, soul, and mind?

5. What does it mean to love your neighbor as yourself?

6. Ask the Lord to lead you to someone who needs prayer ministry.

- Open your pray session by having the person close his or her eyes to help the individual focus on the Holy Spirit's presence within, then lead him or her in praying out loud the following prayer: "In the name of Jesus, I bind all distractions and Satan's influence over my mind, will, and emotions. Holy Spirit, I yield to the power of Your control and receive Your presence into the places where I have been double-minded and have not really believed the truth. I choose to lay down all of my self-defense mechanisms and let You into the deep places of unresolved pain and confusion, where I felt alone and did not really know that You were there. Jesus, show me where I am angry, have shut You out, and am functioning independently apart from You. Father God, I need You to hold and comfort me in these wounded places. I surrender all anxiety about the future and bind the power of fear. Amen."

- Instruct the person to stay focused with the intent of listening to the Lord. Have the person ask, "Jesus, what is it that You want to do right now?"

- Ask the person to report back to you, while staying focused in prayer, what he or she might be sensing, seeing, or hearing in the spirit.

- If the Holy Spirit highlights a specific painful memory, ask the person to share how he or she was feeling when the event took place.

- After the person is able to feel and express the pain, encourage him or her to invite Jesus into the memory and reveal any lies that were believed because of the trauma.

- Ask the person if he or she is willing to repent for believing the lie, and then ask Jesus to reveal the truth and His perspective about what happened.

- If the person is holding on to unforgiveness, encourage him or her to cancel the debt and release the offense to Jesus.

- Write down what happened during your prayer session.

7. What insights have you gained from this chapter? Give an example of how you might apply what you learned to your life.

# Appendix: Emotional Pain Words[39]

Abandoned

Accused

Afraid

All my fault

Alone

Angry

Anxious

Apathetic

Ashamed

Bad

Belittled

Betrayal

Betrayed

Bitter

Blamed

Can't do anything
 right

Can't trust
 anyone

Cheap

Cheated

Condemned

Confused

Conspired against

Controlled

Cut off

Deceived

Defeated

Defenseless

Defrauded

Degraded

Desires were
 rejected

Despair

Destroyed

Devalued

Didn't belong

Didn't measure
 up

Dirty

Disappointed

Disgusted

Disrespected

Dominated

Embarrassed

Empty

Exposed

Failure

Fear

Foolish

Forced

Frustrated

Good for nothing

Guilty

Hate myself

Hated

Helpless

Hollow

Hopeless

Humiliated

Hurt

Hysterical

Impure

Inadequate

Indecent

Inferior

Insecure

Insensitive to my
 needs

Insignificant

Invalidated

Left out

Lied to

Lonely

Lost

Made fun of

Manipulated

Mindless

Mistreated

Misunderstood

Molested

Neglected

No good

Not being
 affirmed

Not cared for

Not cherished

Not deserving
 to live

Not listened to

Not measuring up

Not valued

Opinions not
 valued

Out of control

Overwhelmed

Pathetic

Pressure to
 perform

Pressured

Publicly shamed

Rejected

Rejection

Repulsed

Revenge

Ruined

Sad

Scared

Secluded

Self-disgust

Shamed

Stressed

Stupid

Suffocated

Suicidal

Taken advantage
 of

Thwarted

Torn apart

Trapped

Trash

Ugly

Unable to
 communicate

Unaccepted

Uncared for

Uncaring

Unchosen

Unclean

Unfairly judged

Unfairly treated

Unfit

Unimportant

Unlovable

Unloved

Unnecessary

Unprotected

Unsafe

Unsympathetic

Unwanted

Used

Violated

Vulnerable

Wasted

Wicked

Worthless

Wounded

# End Notes

[1] The Life Model: Living from the Heart Jesus Gave You, James G. Friesen *et al,* Shepherd's House, Inc., page 12 – 13

[2] Biblical Concepts Counseling Workbook, John Regier, Caring for the Heart Ministries, 1999, page 129

[3] Ibid, Regier, page 136

[4] Courageous Conversations Guide, Chris Hogan, Noble Call Institute, 2005 (noblecall.org/articles/partner/the-10-questions-of-a-courageous-conversation/)

[5] The New King James version of the Bible has been used exclusively throughout this workbook.

[6] There Were Two Trees in the Garden, Rick Joyner, Morningstar Publications, 1992, page 9

[7] Ibid, Joyner, page 10

[8] More Tools for Liberating the Bruised, Dr. Joe and Rita Albright, Smooth Sailing Press, 2011, page 55

[9] Ibid, Albright, page 131

[10] Ibid, Albright, page 129

[11] Ibid, Albright, page 93

[12] Ibid, Albright, page 130

[13] Ibid, Albright, page 132

[14] Restoring Shattered Lives, Dr. Tom and Diane Hawkins, Restoration in Christ Ministries, 2006, page 77

[15] Ibid, Albright, page 132

[16] Ibid, Regier, page 60

[17] Ibid, Regier, page 60

[18] Ibid, Regier, page 63

[19] Ibid, Regier, page 60

[20] The Calvary Road, Roy Hession, Christian Literature Crusade, 1950, page 22

[21] Ibid, Hession, page 23

[22] Ibid, Regier, page 62

[23] Ibid, Hession, page 24

[24] Ibid, Hession, page 25

[25] Ibid, Hession, page 28

[26] The Blood of the Cross, Andrew Murray, Whitaker House, 1981, page 31

[27] Ibid, Murray, pages 31-32

[28] Ibid, Murray, page 33

[29] Ibid, Regier, page 33

[30] Thrive – Changing My Generation, Year Three Advanced Skill Training, Chris and Jennifer Coursey, Shepherd's House Inc., 2009, page 5.

[31] The Way of the Heart, Henri J.M. Nouwen, Harper Collins, 1981, page 76

[32] Ibid, Nouwen, pages 78-79

[33] Communion with God, Destiny Image, 1983, pages 47-48

[34] How We Love, Milan and Kay Yerkovich, Water Brook Press, 2008, pages 50- 51

[35] Restoring Shattered Lives, Dr. Tom and Diane Hawkins, Restoration in Christ Ministries, 2006, page 110

[36] Ibid, Hawkins, page 108

[37] Ibid, Hawkins, page 98

[38] Ibid, Regier, page 71

[39] Ibid, Regier, page 30

# Check Out Our Other Coloring Books

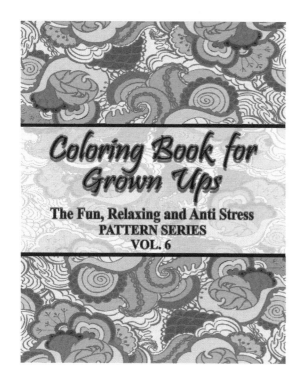

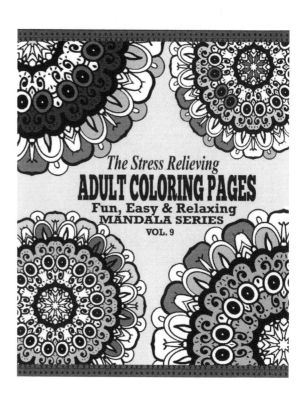

Made in the USA
San Bernardino, CA
26 December 2015